Bugs, Bugs, Bugs!

Centipedes

by Margaret Hall

Consulting Editor: Gail Saunders-Smith, PhD

Consultant: Laura Jesse, Extension Associate
Department of Entomology
Iowa State University
Ames, Iowa

Capstone
press

Mankato, Minnesota

Pebble Plus is published by Capstone Press,
151 Good Counsel Drive, P.O. Box 669, Mankato, Minnesota 56002.
www.capstonepress.com

1 2 3 4 5 6 11 10 09 08 07 06

Library of Congress Cataloging-in-Publication Data
Hall, Margaret, 1947–
     Centipedes / by Margaret Hall.
     p. cm.—(Pebble plus. Bugs, bugs, bugs!)
     Summary: "Simple text and photographs present centipedes, how they look, and what they do"
—Provided by publisher.
     Includes bibliographical references and index.
     ISBN-13: 978-0-7368-5348-4 (hardcover)
     ISBN-10: 0-7368-5348-0 (hardcover)
     1. Centipedes—Juvenile literature. I. Title. II. Series.
QL449.5.H25 2006
595.6'2—dc22   2005023720

Editorial Credits
Mari C. Schuh, editor; Linda Clavel, set designer; Kia Adams, book designer; Jo Miller, photo researcher;
     Scott Thoms, photo editor

Photo Credits
Bill Beatty, 14–15
Bruce Coleman Inc., 9; Jane Burton, 17; John Bell, 1
Corbis/Frank Lane Picture Agency/B. Borrell Casals, 18–19; Chris Mattison, 13;
     Gallo Images/Anthony Bannister, 6–7
Corel, back cover
James P. Rowan, 21
Peter Arnold Inc./James Gerholdt, 5; Matt Meadows, cover; Tom Vezo, 10–11

Note to Parents and Teachers

The Bugs, Bugs, Bugs! set supports national science standards related to the diversity
of life and heredity. This book describes and illustrates centipedes. The images support
early readers in understanding the text. The repetition of words and phrases helps early
readers learn new words. This book also introduces early readers to subject-specific
vocabulary words, which are defined in the Glossary section. Early readers may need
assistance to read some words and to use the Table of Contents, Glossary, Read More,
Internet Sites, and Index sections of the book.

Table of Contents

What Are Centipedes?

Centipedes are small animals

with many legs.

Centipedes have

long, flat bodies.

Centipedes live in dark places.

They crawl around at night.

How Centipedes Look

Most centipedes are the size
of a paper clip.
Some centipedes are
as long as an adult's foot.

9

Most centipedes have
brown, black, or yellow bodies.
Some centipedes
are bright colors.

Centipedes have hard bodies
with many sections.
Each section has two legs.
Their front legs have claws
with poison.

What Centipedes Do

Female centipedes
lay eggs in dirt or wood.
Some females curl around
the eggs to keep them safe.

Young centipedes shed
their skin as they grow.
They grow new legs
each time they shed.

17

Centipedes use their antennas to find prey. Then they poison their prey. Centipedes eat worms, insects, and other small animals.

Centipedes have

two back legs that act

like antennas.

They sense danger

and keep the centipede safe.

Glossary

female—animal that can be a mother

poison—a liquid that can hurt or kill animals and people

prey—an animal that is hunted and eaten by another animal; frogs, mice, and lizards are prey of large centipedes.

shed—to get rid of

Read More

Merrick, Patrick. *Centipedes.* Naturebooks. Chanhassen, Minn.: Child's World, 2003.

Morgan, Sally. *Spiders, Centipedes, and Millipedes.* Looking at Minibeasts. North Mankato, Minn.: Thameside Press, 2000.

Povey, Karen D. *Centipede.* Bugs. San Diego: Kidhaven Press, 2004.

Internet Sites

FactHound offers a safe, fun way to find Internet sites related to this book. All of the sites on FactHound have been researched by our staff.

Here's how:

1. Visit *www.facthound.com*

2. Type in this special code **0736853480** for age-appropriate sites. Or enter a search word related to this book for a more general search.

3. Click on the **Fetch It** button.

FactHound will fetch the best sites for you!

Index

Word Count: 143
Grade: 1
Early-Intervention Level: 14